Marilyn Conroy-Schulz

Two Pantomimes for Christmas

Jack and the Beanstalk

and

Dick Whittington

Ernst Klett Verlag
Stuttgart Düsseldorf Leipzig

Gedruckt auf Recyclingpapier,
hergestellt aus 100 % Altpapier.

1. Auflage A 1 5 4 3 2 1 2004 2003 2002 2001 2000

Alle Drucke dieser Auflage können im Unterricht nebeneinander benutzt werden. Die letzte Zahl bezeichnet das Jahr dieses Druckes.

Internetadresse: http://www.klett-verlag.de

Umschlag/Illustrationen: Duncan Smith, London.
Druck: Druckhaus Vogel GmbH, Leinfelden-Echterdingen
Printed in Germany.
ISBN 3-12-571414-1

Contents

Introduction

Liebe Schülerinnen und Schüler,

eine Pantomime gehört für jedes englische Kind zu den unverzichtbaren Freuden der Weihnachtszeit. Allerdings ist eine Pantomime in England nicht – wie in Deutschland – ein Theaterstück, bei dem nur gespielt und nicht gesprochen wird. In England ist es eher eine Art Musical, dessen Inhalt auf einem der vielen englischen und deutschen Märchen basiert. Diese Art von Theaterstück hat eine lange Tradition und, wie gesagt, zur Weihnachtszeit wird in jeder englischen Stadt, die ein Theater hat, auch eine Pantomime aufgeführt.
In jeder *Pantomime* gibt es einige festgelegte Charaktere: eine lustige alte Frau (meistens von einem Mann gespielt, der als Frau verkleidet und gut ausgepolstert ist) und ein Liebespaar, bei dem der Junge meistens von einem Mädchen gespielt wird (wegen der hübscheren Beine). Natürlich gibt es auch immer einen Bösewicht (im ersten Stück der *Giant* und im zweiten *King Rat*), den die Zuschauer – von denen erwartet wird, dass sie "mitgehen" – bei jedem Erscheinen auf der Bühne auspfeifen, während sie den guten Jüngling (*Jack* bzw. *Dick*) anfeuern, wenn er in Gefahr gerät. Und schließlich gibt es auch noch einen Tölpel (*Ruby* bzw. *Polly*), den man mit reinem Gewissen auslachen kann.
Beim Vorbereiten einer Aufführung sind nicht nur die Schauspieler und die Helfer hinter der Bühne beteiligt, sondern die ganze Klasse, die mit Ideen und Anregungen die Aufführung zu einem Erfolg werden lassen kann.
Ihr alle könnt mithelfen, zum Beispiel bei der Auswahl der Musikeinlagen. Diese können sich ganz nach dem Geschmack eurer Klasse richten. Aus den englischen und amerikanischen Hitparaden sucht ihr beliebte und bekannte Lieder aus, fügt sie in passende Stellen des Stückes ein und tragt sie im Playback-Verfahren vor.
Es ist immer wieder erstaunlich, was für eine Phantasie Schülerinnen und Schüler entwickeln, wenn es um die Fragen der

Kostüme, des Bühnenaufbaus und der Requisiten geht. Die *Widow Twanky* (in *Jack and the Beanstalk*) haben wir immer so kunstvoll mit Kissen ausgepolstert, dass sie wirklich wie eine behäbige Bauersfrau aussah (mit *Mrs Shufflebottom* in *Dick Whittington* kann man es genauso machen); und die Harfe bekam goldene Bänder an ihren ausgestreckten rechten Arm gebunden, die unten zusammen am rechten Fuß befestigt wurden!

Das größte Problem in *Jack and the Beanstalk* schien am Anfang die Bohnenranke zu sein, an der der Held des Stückes zu dem Schloss des Riesen hinaufklettern kann. Aber dieses Problem wurde schließlich ganz einfach gelöst, nämlich mit einer Stehleiter. Sie stand ganz am seitlichen Rand der Bühne, halb verdeckt durch den Vorhang. Der sichtbare Teil der Leiter war mit Zweigen und Blättern so umwunden, dass das Ganze wirklich fast wie echt aussah.

Und der Backofen, in dem Jack sich versteckt? Das Huhn, das goldene Eier legt? Und *King Rat* und seine Rattenbande und die erstaunliche Katze *Puss* in *Dick Whittington*? Mit Pappe und Bastelpapier, mit Kleber und Schminke werdet ihr sicherlich alle diese Fragen lösen und auch sonst noch viele eigene Ideen für die Gestaltung der Bühne haben.

Wir haben diese Stücke mit verschiedenen Klassen für unsere Eltern und Geschwister aufgeführt oder auch für jüngere Schüler. Deswegen haben wir, zum besseren Verständnis der Stücke, einen Erzähler (*storyteller*) eingeführt, der vor jeder Szene mit ein paar deutschen Sätzen einen Überblick über die folgende Handlung gibt.

Wir, Schüler und Lehrer, haben mit diesen *Pantomimes* sehr viel Spaß gehabt (besonders die Schüler, wenn ein Lehrer die Rolle des Bösewichts (*Giant*) übernahm, und man ihn dann so richtig ausbuhen konnte!). Indem wir euch hier *Jack and the Beanstalk* und *Dick Whittington* vorstellen, möchten wir unsere Freude am Theaterspielen mit euch teilen.

Viel Spaß bei der Vorbereitung und bei der Aufführung!

Marilyn Conroy-Schulz
(St. Joseph-Gymnasium, Rheinbach)

Jack and the Beanstalk

A pantomime in 9 scenes

Characters:
Storyteller
Jack (acted by a girl)
His girlfriend, Marian
His mother, Widow Twanky (acted by a boy)
Daisy, the cow
The Giant
The Giant's wife
The servant, Ruby
The golden harp
The hen that lays golden eggs
An old man
The fishseller
The greengrocer
A lady
A pie-man

1 **beanstalk**	Bohnenranke/Bohnenpflanze
7 **widow** ['wɪdəʊ]	Witwe
9 **giant** ['dʒaɪənt]	Riese
11 **servant**	Diener/in
12 **harp**	Harfe
13 **to lay eggs**	Eier legen
16 **greengrocer** ['gri:nˌgrəʊsə]	Obst- und Gemüsehändler
18 **pie-man** ['paɪmən]	ein Bauchladenverkäufer, der leckere Pasteten (*pies*) anbietet

Prologue

The storyteller steps in front of the curtain.

Sehr geehrtes Publikum!

Mit unserem Theaterstück wollen wir Sie jetzt in eine Zeit entführen, in der es in England noch Riesen und Zauberbohnen gab und auch Hühner, die goldene Eier legten.
Unser Stück heißt *Jack and the Beanstalk – Jack und die Bohnenranke*. Das ist ein bekanntes englisches Märchen, das wir in eine *Pantomime* verwandeln.
Eine *Pantomime* ist nicht – wie in Deutschland – ein Stück, bei dem nur gespielt und nicht gesprochen wird. Eine *Pantomime* ist in England ein Märchen, das als Theaterstück gespielt wird, meistens zur Weihnachtszeit.
In jeder *Pantomime* gibt es einige festgelegte Charaktere: einen Bösewicht, eine lustige alte Frau (meistens von einem Mann gespielt) und ein Liebespaar, bei dem der Junge meistens von einem Mädchen gespielt wird – wegen der hübscheren Beine.
Alle diese Charaktere werden Sie auch in unserem Stück wiederfinden.
Bei einer *Pantomime* wird erwartet, dass das Publikum "mitmacht". Sie dürfen den Bösewicht ruhig ausbuhen und den guten Jüngling lautstark anfeuern, wenn er in Gefahr gerät.

Das Stück beginnt im Kuhstall der armen Witwe Twanky. Sie versucht ihre Kuh Daisy zu melken und ist ganz verzweifelt, weil diese keine Milch mehr geben will. Auch ihr Sohn Jack hat beim Melken keinen Erfolg, obwohl ihm seine Freundin Marian dabei hilft. Schließlich geben sie auf, und die Mutter schickt Jack zum Markt, um Daisy zu verkaufen, weil sie Geld für Lebensmittel brauchen.

Scene 1: Widow Twanky's dairy

Jack's mother, Widow Twanky, is talking to the cow.

MOTHER: (*to cow*) It's time you gave us some milk, you silly old cow.

Enter Jack with Marian, hand in hand.

MOTHER: Come on you two! Stop that nonsense! It's time to milk old Daisy here. I hope she gives us some milk today. (*Taking out her purse*) I must go to market to buy bread and this is all the money I have! I hope there will be some milk to sell. Come on Jack, get the stool and start to milk her.

Jack brings the stool and starts to milk. Marian goes to stroke the cow's head.

JACK: (*to cow*) Come on Daisy. You can do better than this! ...

MOTHER: What shall we do, what shall we do? You silly old cow, you are not worth the grass you eat in the field!

JACK: (*to mother*) It's no use. This is all she can give us (*shows milk*).

MOTHER: What shall we do, what shall we do?

JACK: Never mind, Mother, I'll go and get some work somewhere.

MOTHER: You? Get work? No, no, we've tried that before! It's no use, you must take her to market and sell her. (*Jack takes Marian*) – No, no! Not Marian – the cow, you idiot!

JACK: All right, mother, it's market day today, and I'll soon sell Daisy and then we'll see what we can do.

MARIAN: I am sorry, Jack, I can't come with you. I must go and help my mother in the garden.

1	**dairy** ['deərɪ]	Kuhstall; Molkerei
10	**stool**	Schemel
11	**to stroke**	streicheln
15	**worth** [wɜːθ]	wert

JACK: Never mind, Marian, I can go alone, see you later. Bye, Marian! Bye, mother! Come on Daisy, you old fool!

Exit all.

(Storyteller explains the next scene.)

Scene 2: Market

Fishseller and greengrocer at their stalls; the pie-man is walking around. People are looking and buying things.

FISHSELLER: Fresh fish! Fresh fish! Caught this morning in the deep blue sea! They are ready to jump in the pan for you! Watch them wiggle there! (*shows a wiggling fish*)

GREENGROCER: Apples! Bananas! Here you are! You know what they say – "an apple a day keeps the doctor away"! Come and try them!

PIE-MAN: (*walking around with a tray*) How about a lovely pie? An apple pie? Cheese-and-onion? I've got them all. Freshly baked this morning!

LADY: My goodness, those do look good! Can you give me a nice pork pie for my husband's dinner?

PIE-MAN: Here you are, lady – a *beautiful* pie which I made with my own expert hands.

LADY: Thank you very much. How much does it cost?

PIE-MAN: £1.50.

LADY: Really? So much? Oh, I can't come here very often then.

3 **exit** ['eksɪt]	abgehen (im Theater)
6 **stall**	Stand
10 **to wiggle**	wackeln, zappeln
14 **tray**	Tablett; *hier:* Bauchladen
15 **onion** ['ʌnjən]	Zwiebel
18 **pork**	Schweinefleisch

PIE-MAN: What do you expect, lady? – I bake them with only the finest products.

FISHSELLER: Fresh fish! Fresh fish! How about a nice herring for your old man's tea?

LADY: Well really, I don't know. Are they really fresh?

GREENGROCER: Fresh, he says! Huh! You don't want to buy from him! The whole lot stinks to high heaven! Have a sniff! (*lady sniffs*) No! No! Why don't you cook some of my wonderful vegetables for your old man? They're fresh from the garden this morning. Look at them! Why, I give you only the best here! How about it, lady? Try one of these apples! But watch your false teeth!

(Storyteller explains the next scene.)

Scene 3: On the road to the market

Jack is walking along with the cow.

JACK: (*to cow*) What a lovely day this is! What a pity we must sell you, old girl!

SONG (e.g. "Always look on the bright side of life", Monty Python)

Enter old man.

OLD MAN: Good morning, Jack!

JACK: Good morning to you, sir! How do you know my name?

OLD MAN: Aha! I know many things that you don't know! Where are you off to now?

1	**to expect**	erwarten
4	**tea**	*hier:* Abendessen
7	**to stink to high heaven** ['hevn]	wie die Pest stinken
7	**to sniff**	schnuppern
11	**false teeth**	Gebiss, Zahnprothese
22	**sir**	höfliche Anrede für einen älteren Mann

JACK: I'm going to the market to sell our cow here.

OLD MAN: Oh, yes. You just look the right sort of young man to sell a cow. I wonder if you know how many beans make five?

JACK: Two in each hand and one in your mouth!

OLD MAN: Right you are! (*slapping him on the back*) and here they are, the very beans themselves! (*He pulls out a bag of beans.)* As you are so clever – I don't mind doing a swap with you, your cow for these beans!

JACK: Go along, wouldn't you like it?

OLD MAN: Ah! You don't know what these beans are. If you plant them overnight, by morning they will grow up to the sky. They are very special beans, they are magic beans!

JACK: Really, you don't say!

OLD MAN: I do say! And if it doesn't turn out to be true, you can have your cow back.

JACK: Great! I can't do anything wrong here! Here you are! (*handing over Daisy*) Give me the beans!

(Storyteller explains the next scene.)

Scene 4: Widow Twanky's cottage.

Jack enters.

JACK: Hello, Mother!

MOTHER: Well, well, well! Back already, Jack? I see you haven't got Daisy with you, so you've sold her?

JACK: You'll never guess, Mother, you'll never guess.

5 **to slap**	(mit der flachen Hand) schlagen
6 **the very beans**	die echten Bohnen
7 **swap** [swɒp]	Tausch
12 **magic** ['mædʒɪk]	Zauber-
14 **to turn out**	*hier:* sich herausstellen
19 **cottage** ['kɒtɪdʒ]	Häuschen (auf dem Lande)
24 **to guess** [ges]	raten

MOTHER: No, boy, good lad, now come on, tell me, how much did you get? Ten pounds, – fifteen pounds, – twenty pounds – ! No – it couldn't be thirty pounds?

JACK: I told you you couldn't guess. What do you say to these – these beans – look! They're magical, plant them overnight and ...

MOTHER: What?! No! I can't believe this. Have you been such an idiot as to give away my wonderful Daisy, my queen of cows, the best milker in the village for a bag of ... of ... of ... stupid beans? Take that ... and that ... and that (*hitting him and chasing him round the audience*). As for your stupid beans, here they go out of the window (*throws them out of the window*). And now off with you to bed! Not a bite to eat shall you have tonight, not a drop to drink! ...

JACK: Mother! ... please, Mother ...!

MOTHER: Don't talk to me!

Jack gets sadly into bed.

SONG (e.g. Blues)

(Storyteller explains the next scene.)

Scene 5: Jack's room

JACK: (*yawning*) Oh dear, what a night! Nothing to eat and nothing to drink! What time is it? – Eight o'clock? But why is it so dark in here? – Hey, what's this? These great big leaves? What is all this? – No, it can't be? It's a huge beanstalk! Enormous! It stretches from there in the garden to ... to... I don't know where!

9	**to chase** [tʃeɪs]	jagen
10	**as ... for**	was ... betrifft
12	**bite** [baɪt]	Bissen
13	**drop**	Tropfen
20	**to yawn** [jɔːn]	gähnen
24	**to stretch**	sich strecken, reichen

It's so big and strong! I wonder if I can climb it and see?

He tries the beanstalk and starts climbing.

JACK: Hey, where am I? This is a very strange place indeed. There is a great castle over there! I think I'll go over and see who lives there.

Curtain.

(Storyteller explains the next scene.)

Scene 6: Giant's castle

Jack goes to the door and knocks; the giant's wife opens the door.

JACK : (*bowing*) Good morning, ma'am. Could you please give me some breakfast? I haven't had anything to eat for such a long time and I'm *so* hungry!

GIANT'S WIFE: It's breakfast you want, is it? It is breakfast you'll *be* if you don't move off from here quick! My husband is a giant who likes nothing better for breakfast than little boys – on toast! You must go as quick as you can or he'll soon be here.

JACK: Oh, please, ma'am, – please give me something to eat. I've had nothing to eat since yesterday morning, really and truly, ma'am! It is just as bad to die of hunger as to die on toast as somebody's breakfast.

GIANT'S WIFE: Oh, well then – Ruby (*to servant*) – Ruby! Give him some bread and cheese and a jug of milk! – But make sure you are quick, my boy, my husband will be back soon and he'll be very hungry, too.

1 **to wonder** sich fragen
11 **to bow** [baʊ] sich verbeugen
11 **ma'am** (= madam) sehr höfliche Anrede für eine Dame

Ruby scratches her head and fetches something to eat, falling over her own feet as she does so. Jack eats hungrily. After a while they all hear the noise of the giant.

GIANT'S WIFE: Oh my goodness, it's my old man back! What on earth shall we do? Come on, Ruby! Help me! Let's stuff him in the oven.

They quickly push him in the oven. – Enter giant wearing hens and rabbits in his belt. He throws these on the table.

GIANT: Here you are, wife, you can boil these up for breakfast – but wait (*sniffing*) – what's this I smell (*sniffing*)?

Fee – fi – fo –fum (*sniffing*)!
I smell the blood of an Englishman!
Be he alive or be he dead,
I'll have his bones to grind my bread!

Ruby's mouth drops open in shock and she starts to look frightened.

GIANT'S WIFE: Nonsense dear, you're dreaming. Or perhaps you smell the scraps of that little boy you liked so much for yesterday's dinner. Here – you go and have a wash and tidy-up and by the time you come back, your breakfast'll be ready.

Giant goes out – Jack opens the oven door and wants to escape. Ruby looks shocked.

RUBY: No, no, it's too dangerous! Wait till he's asleep! He always has a sleep after breakfast.

5	**to stuff**	stopfen
6	**oven** [ʌvn]	(Back-)Ofen
13	**be he** ...(*lit.*)	if he is ...
13	**alive**	lebendig, lebend
14	**to grind** [graɪnd]	mahlen
18	**scraps**	(Über-)Reste

Jack goes back to the oven. Giant enters and eats. Giant's wife and Ruby serve him. Then they leave. He takes up a couple of bags of gold from the corner. He sits and counts the money until his head begins to nod and he snores loudly. Jack comes out of the oven – goes over on tiptoe and takes one of the bags and runs off.

(Storyteller explains the next scene.)

Scene 7: The cottage

Jack is showing the gold to Marian and Widow Twanky.

JACK: See, Mother, I told you those were magic beans! Isn't this wonderful! We're rich!

MARIAN: Oh Jack, now we can get married!

SONG (e.g. love song from the hitparade)

MOTHER: Married? What's this "married"? Oh no, first we must start to put the farm in order and buy a few nice things for the house and a few nice clothes for me before you can get ideas about getting married. Come on now – let's have a bit of action!

She drags Marian off.

JACK: I *knew* Mother would take all my money! I think I must try my luck again. (*To audience*) What do *you* think? Shall I go up the beanstalk? (*Nodding*) Yes? – or shall I not? (*shaking his head*)

4	**to nod**	nicken
4	**to snore** [snɔː]	schnarchen
5	**to go on tiptoe**	auf Zehenspitzen gehen
12	**to get married**	heiraten
18	**to drag s.o. off**	jemanden wegschleppen
19	**to try one's luck**	sein Glück versuchen

He goes off to climb the beanstalk.

(Storyteller explains the next scene.)

Scene 8: The Giant's castle

Jack is knocking at the door. Giant's wife opens the door; Ruby cowers behind her – she looks pleased to see Jack.

JACK: Good morning, ma'am. Could you please give me something to eat?

GIANT'S WIFE: Go away, my boy, or my husband will eat you up for breakfast. But aren't you the boy who came here once before? Do you know, that very day my husband missed one of his bags of gold?

JACK: That's very strange, ma'am. I expect I could tell you something about that but I'm so hungry I can't speak about it until I've had something to eat.

GIANT'S WIFE: Oh, all right, then! Ruby, bring him some bread and cheese and a jug of milk. (*Jack eats hungrily*) But make sure you're quick, boy.

The noise of the giant! The wife quickly runs to fetch his breakfast. Ruby wants to hide Jack in the oven again but he refuses and hides behind a curtain. Enter giant and wife with breakfast tray.

GIANT: Fee – fi – fo – fum (*sniffing*)!
I smell the blood of an Englishman!
Be he alive or be he dead,
I'll have his bones to grind my bread!

GIANT'S WIFE: Now don't start that again. Here, come and have your breakfast.

5 **to cower** ['kaʊə] sich ducken, kauern
19 **to refuse** [rɪ'fjuːz] sich weigern

The giant eats and Ruby and his wife serve him.

GIANT: Wife, bring me the hen that lays the golden eggs!

The wife brings the hen.

GIANT: Now – lay, hen, lay!

The hen squawks and lays a golden egg.

GIANT: Now bring me my golden harp to sing me a lullaby. – sing, harp, sing!

Ruby and the wife bring the golden harp which begins to sing.

HARP MUSIC

Ruby and the wife exit. The giant begins to fall asleep and snore. Jack tiptoes out and takes the golden harp and the golden hen and leaves. They both make a noise on their way out, waking the giant.

GIANT: (*waking*) What's this? What's this? Where's my wonderful hen? Where is my golden harp? Wife? Wife? What's happening?

WIFE: (*entering*) Oh husband! What's the matter? – It's that boy, I'm sure. I put him in the oven ready for lunch. (*She looks*) No, it's empty. Where can he be? – There he is!

They all chase after him, round the room. They come to the beanstalk. Jack pushes the harp and the hen down and picks up an axe and chops the beanstalk down. The giant and his wife can go no further.

5	**to squawk** [skwɔ:k]	gackern
6	**lullaby** ['lʌləbaɪ]	Wiegenlied
10	**to fall asleep**	einschlafen
16	**what's the matter?**	was ist los?
21	**axe**	Axt
21	**to chop s.th. down**	fällen

(Storyteller explains the next scene.)

Scene 9: The cottage

Jack with the hen and the harp.

JACK: (*to Mother and Marian*) Oh, that was a near thing! My goodness – I thought that was the end!
MARIAN: Oh my poor darling! Are you all right?

SONG (e.g. love song from the hitparade)

MOTHER: You silly idiot! What have you got with you this time, a hen and a harp?
JACK: This is not just any hen! – Wait! Lay, hen, lay!

The hen lays a golden egg.

MOTHER: Hey, not bad – Can I try? – Lay, hen, lay!

The hen lays another golden egg.

MARIAN: Can I have a go? – Lay, hen, lay! (*hen lays an egg*)
ALL TOGETHER: We're rich!! We're rich!
MOTHER: I can't believe it!
MARIAN: Jack, give me a kiss!

SONG (e.g. "We are the champions" – Queen)

THE END

4 **that was a near thing!** das war knapp!
14 **to have a go** etwas probieren, versuchen

The storyteller's text

Scene 2

Während Jack sich auf den Weg zur Stadt macht, herrscht dort reges Markttreiben. Ein Fischhändler, ein Gemüseverkäufer und ein Pastetenbäcker versuchen sich gegenseitig die Kunden abspenstig zu machen.

Scene 3

Auf seinem Weg zur Stadt trifft Jack einen geheimnisvollen Mann. Dieser will seine Kuh haben und bietet ihm dafür Zauberbohnen an. Jack zögert. Aber als der Fremde ihm klarmacht, dass es sich hier tatsächlich um Zauberbohnen handelt, die in einer Nacht bis zum Himmel wachsen, stimmt er dem Tausch zu.

Scene 4

Jack macht sich überglücklich auf den Heimweg und kann es kaum erwarten, seiner Mutter die Zauberbohnen zu zeigen. Aber diese scheint gar nicht sehr erfreut darüber. Wütend schmeißt sie die Bohnen aus dem Fenster. Jack bezieht eine Tracht Prügel und muss ohne Abendessen ins Bett gehen.

Scene 5

Als Jack am nächsten Morgen aufwacht, erwartet ihn eine außergewöhnliche Überraschung: Vor seinem Fenster ist über Nacht eine mächtige Pflanze gewachsen, eine riesige Kletterbohne. Sie reicht weit bis in den Himmel! Welcher Junge würde da nicht sofort hochklettern wollen!

Scene 6

Jack klettert an der riesigen Bohnenranke hoch und landet vor einer großen Tür. Eine Frau öffnet ihm, und er bettelt – verzweifelt vor Hunger – um ein Frühstück. Das bekommt er dann auch. Aber die Frau warnt ihn vor ihrem Mann, denn der ist ein Riese und liebt zum Frühstück kleine Jungen – auf Toast! Als der Riese dann wirklich erscheint, ist guter Rat teuer. Jack muss sich im Backofen verstecken. Der Riese glaubt, einen Menschen zu riechen, aber seiner Frau gelingt es, ihn abzulenken. Erst als der Riese gespeist hat und danach beim Zählen seines Goldes einschläft, kann Jack sich aus seinem Versteck wagen und über die Bohnenleiter wieder auf die Erde klettern, aber nicht ohne einen der Goldsäcke des Riesen mitzunehmen.

Scene 7
Jack kehrt heim und zeigt überglücklich das Gold. Seine Freundin Marian hört bereits die Hochzeitsglocken läuten, aber die Mutter hat andere Vorstellungen von der Verwendung des Geldes. Jack überlegt, ob er noch einmal die Zauberbohnenranke hochklettern und sein Glück versuchen soll.

Scene 8
Wieder gelangt Jack zur Wohnung des Riesen. Dessen Frau ist aber diesmal deutlich unfreundlicher, denn sie verdächtigt Jack, einen Beutel Gold gestohlen zu haben. Aber trotz dieses Verdachtes servieren sie und ihre Magd Ruby dem jungen Gast ein Essen. Wieder erscheint der Riese! Wieder riecht er einen Menschen und will ihn verspeisen. Und wieder gelingt es seiner Frau, ihn abzulenken. Nach dem Essen verlangt der Riese nach seinem Huhn, das ihm goldene Eier legt, und als ihm dann seine goldene Harfe vorspielt, schläft er selig ein. Jack will diese Situation nutzen, um sich wieder in Sicherheit zu bringen. Als er aber das Huhn ergreift und auch noch die Harfe mitnehmen will, macht er zu viel Lärm und weckt den Riesen. Es beginnt eine aufregende Jagd, bei der der Riese und seine Frau Jack fast erwischen.

Scene 9
Nur ganz knapp konnte Jack entkommen. Er, seine Mutter und Marian finden Gefallen an der Henne, die goldene Eier legt, und als sie begreifen, dass sie nun reich sind, steht auch einer Hochzeit nichts mehr im Wege.

Questions and exercises

Scene 1: Widow Twanky's dairy

A: Which is right?

1. Widow Twanky is angry because
   a) Jack has forgotten to milk Daisy
   b) Daisy does not give much milk
   c) the milkman has not brought the milk
   d) the milk has gone sour.

2. Widow Twanky wants to go to market because
   a) she must buy some milk
   b) she wants to sell some cakes
   c) she must buy some bread
   d) she wants to buy a new cow.

3. Jack thinks it is a good idea
   a) to sell Daisy at the market
   b) to help his mother in the house
   c) to help Marian's mother in the garden
   d) to sell milk at the market.

B: Answer the questions

1) Jack has a cow – What other words for animals do you know? Make a list and compare it with your partner's.
2) Marian must help her mother in the garden. What must *you* do to help at home?

wash the dishes? make the beds? set the table?
go shopping? clean the windows? do the ironing?
cut the grass? make the breakfast? etc.

Scene 2: The market

A: Which is right?

1. The fishseller is selling
   a) fish and chips
   b) fresh fish
   c) fish for the aquarium.

2. The greengrocer is selling
   a) apples and pears
   b) apples and oranges
   c) apples and bananas.

3. The pie-man is selling
   a) apple pies, cream cakes and bread
   b) apple pies, pork pies and cheese-and-onion pies
   c) apple pies, fish pies and pork pies

4. The lady thinks that the pie-man's pies are
   a) very cheap
   b) very bad
   c) very expensive.

B: Answer the questions

1) This is a market in the Middle Ages. What names of shops and buildings in a modern town do you know? Make a list.
2) Make a shopping-list of six things which you must buy for your mum.

Scene 3: On the road to market

A: Are these sentences right or wrong? If they are wrong, correct them.

1. The old man does not know Jack's name.
2. Jack is on his way to market to go shopping for his mother.
3. Jack knows how to count five beans.
4. The old man wants to buy the cow from Jack.
5. If Jack plants the beans, they will grow very quickly.
6. Jack thinks it is a silly idea to swap a cow for a bag of beans.

B: Answer the questions

1) What does the old man tell his wife when he arrives back home with the cow? Write down their conversation.
2) Do you ever swap things with your friends? Say what you think are three fair swaps.

Scenes 4 and 5: Widow Twanky's cottage; Jack's room

A: Which is right?

1. Widow Twanky is very angry because
   a) Jack has forgotten to buy some things at the market
   b) Jack has lost his money at the market
   c) Jack has given the cow away for a bag of beans
   d) Jack has brought the cow back home again.

2. Widow Twanky says that Daisy
   a) was a silly old cow
   b) was a hopeless milker
   c) gave no milk at all
   d) was the best milker in the village.

3. Jack is very sad because he must
   a) go to school without any sandwiches
   b) go to bed without any food or drink
   c) go to market without any money
   d) go to bed without a hot-water bottle.

4. Jack is surprised because the beanstalk
   a) stretches from the garden to the road
   b) has not grown very high
   c) stretches from the garden into the sky
   d) has many red flowers.

B: Answer the questions

1) Jack's mother said he was an idiot. Do you think he was silly to sell the cow for the beans? Give reasons.
2) Have you ever gone to bed without an evening meal? Why?
3) Draw a picture of Jack when he wakes up in bed and sees the beanstalk through the window.

Scene 6: Giant's castle

A: Complete the sentences

1. Jack is so hungry that he asks the giant's wife for some ... .
2. The giant's favourite breakfast is ... .
3. Ruby, the servant, brings Jack some ... to eat and ... to drink.
4. Before the giant comes, Jack must hide in the ... .
5. When the giant comes he thinks he can smell ... .
6. Ruby tells Jack that the giant always ... after breakfast.
7. Before Jack runs off, he takes ... with him.

B: Answer the questions

1) Make a list of all the things you can think of to eat and drink.
2) What do British people have for breakfast?
3) What is *your* favourite breakfast?

Scene 7: The cottage

A: Which is right?

1. When Jack comes back to the cottage he shows his mother
   a) the magic beans
   b) the bag of gold
   c) the beanstalk.
2. Marian is very happy and says that with the money they can
   a) buy some new clothes
   b) go on holiday
   c) get married.
3. When Widow Twanky takes the bag of gold, Jack plans
   a) to go up the beanstalk again
   b) to go down the beanstalk
   c) to go and dig up the beanstalk.

B: Answer the questions

1) Imagine: you have won a lot of money in a lottery. What would you like to do with it?
2) Marian tells her mother about Jack's adventure. What do you think she says? Write down their conversation.

Scenes 8 and 9: The Giant's castle; The cottage

A: Are these sentences right or wrong? If they are wrong, correct them.

1. When the Giant's wife opens the door, Jack asks for a bed for the night.
2. The Giant's wife says that her husband could not find any of his bags of gold since Jack was there.
3. When the Giant comes, Jack hides in the oven again.
4. The Golden Hen lays a golden egg for the Giant.
5. Ruby sings a lullaby for the Giant.

6. Jack runs off with the Golden Harp and a bag of gold.
7. The Giant and his wife cannot follow Jack down the beanstalk.
8. His mother is very angry that he has brought home a hen that lays brown eggs.

B: Answer the questions

1) Imagine: Jack could not cut down the beanstalk and the Giant followed him down to the cottage! Write down the conversation between the Giant and Widow Twanky.
2) Look at the list of adjectives below. Which are right to describe Widow Twanky, Jack, the old man, the Giant, the Giant's wife?

clever	sad	worried	happy	frightened
funny	kind	angry	silly	stupid

Make sentences with the adjectives.
Example: *Jack is sad when his mother sends him to bed.*

After reading the play

1) What did you think of the pantomime?
   I liked/didn't like "Jack and the Beanstalk" because ...
   My favourite character was ... because ...
   The best part was when ...
2) Draw a poster for the pantomime. Hang it up in the classroom and choose the best. You can make a programme too!

Dick Whittington

A pantomime in 10 scenes

Characters:
Dick Whittington (acted by a girl)
Farmer Brown
Fairy Bowbells
Farmer Green and animals
Thief (non-speaking part)
Mr Fitzwarren, a rich merchant
Alice, his daughter
Bread seller
Fruit seller
Boot seller
Scarf seller
Pet seller
Old man at market
Large lady with small husband
Mrs Shufflebottom, the cook (acted by a boy)
Polly, the stupid servant
King Rat and his Rat chorus
Dick's Puss (acted by a girl)
Captain Hornblower
The Sultan
The Sultan's wife
Servants
The Grand Vizier
Two sailors
Two people to carry signs

6	**fairy**	Fee
9	**merchant** ['mɜ:rtʃənt]	Kaufmann
19	**servant**	Bedienstete/r
27	**sailor**	Matrose

Prologue

The storyteller steps in front of the curtain.

Sehr geehrtes Publikum!

Mit unserem Theaterstück wollen wir Sie jetzt in eine Zeit entführen, in der in England ein armer Junge vom Lande Bürgermeister von London werden konnte, weil es noch gute Feen gab, die ihm in schwierigen Lebenslagen zu Hilfe kamen.

Unser Stück heißt *Dick Whittington.* Das ist ein bekanntes englisches Märchen, das aber einen wahren Kern hat. Dick Whittington hat es wirklich gegeben. Er war dreimal Bürgermeister von London, und liegt auf dem Friedhof von Highgate im Norden von London begraben. Wie er mit Hilfe seiner guten Fee Bowbells Bürgermeister wurde, wollen wir jetzt als *Pantomime* vorspielen.

Eine *Pantomime* ist nicht – wie in Deutschland – ein Stück, bei dem nur gespielt und nicht gesprochen wird. Eine *Pantomime* ist in England ein Märchen, das als Theaterstück gespielt wird, meistens zur Weihnachtszeit.

In jeder *Pantomime* gibt es einige festgelegte Charaktere: einen Bösewicht, eine komische ältere Frau (meistens von einem Mann gespielt), ein dummes Mädchen und ein Liebespaar, bei dem der Junge meistens von einem Mädchen gespielt wird – wegen der hübscheren Beine. Alle diese Charaktere werden Sie auch in diesem Stück wiederfinden.

Bei einer *Pantomime* wird erwartet, dass das Publikum "mitgeht". Sie dürfen den Bösewicht – in unserem Stück *King Rat* (den Rattenkönig) – ruhig ausbuhen und den guten Jüngling – das ist natürlich Dick Whittington – und seine Katze Puss, die ihm zur Seite steht, lautstark anfeuern, wenn er in Gefahr gerät. Und das dumme Mädchen Polly dürfen Sie mit reinem Gewissen auslachen.

Das Stück beginnt vor dem Haus von Farmer Brown. Dick Whittington, ein armer Junge ohne Eltern, hat es nicht leicht im Leben. Er hat Arbeit und Unterkommen bei Farmer Brown gefunden, aber für das harte Landleben scheint er nicht zu taugen, und Farmer Brown verliert seine Geduld mit ihm. Nur Fairy Bowbells, seine gute Fee, kann ihm helfen und rät ihm, nach London zu ziehen, wo es für jeden die Chance auf ein besseres Leben geben soll.

Scene 1: Farmer Brown's farm

Enter Farmer Brown. He carries a sack of potatoes and puts it in the corner. Dick Whittington comes in behind him carrying a sack which seems to be very heavy.

FARMER BROWN: (*Shaking his head*) What am I to do with the harvest so bad this year? No corn to sell and my cows are dying. Then I have workers like you who fall over their own feet if they have to carry a sack of potatoes.

Dick falls under the sack of potatoes.

Get off my land, you good-for-nothing! You're no good for farmwork and I'm tired of giving you food and a bed to sleep on. Be off with you before I use this (*taking a pitchfork*) on your backside!

Farmer Brown chases Dick with the pitchfork round the audience.

6 **harvest** die Ernte
10 **good-for-nothing** Nichtsnutz, Taugenichts
12 **pitchfork** Mistgabels
12 **backside** Hinterteil
14 **to chase** [tʃeɪs] jagen

Curtain – Dick comes in front of the curtain.

DICK: Oh dear! What am I to do with no Mum or Dad to help me and not a friend in the world?

Farmer Brown throws him his stick and bundle from behind the curtain.

SONG (e.g. *Yesterday*, Beatles)

Enter Fairy Bowbells

BOWBELLS: That is not true that you haven't got a friend in the world!

DICK: (*rubbing his eyes*) Who are you? I 've never seen you before.

BOWBELLS: I am your fairy godmother, Bowbells, and I have come to help you and give you some good advice. You poor boy, you mustn't give up hope so soon.

DICK: Oh, Fairy Bowbells, what can I do? I have no home to live in, no family and friends and winter is not very far away!

BOWBELLS: Why don't you leave here and go to London to seek your fortune. London is a wonderful city where everybody can have a chance in life. They say the streets there are paved with gold. (*pointing to Farmer Green*) See, there's a farmer on his way to market there.

Enter Farmer Green with animals.

Why don't you ask him if you can go with him?

DICK: Yes, I think I will. (*to farmer*) Oh please, good sir, if I help you with your animals will you take me with you to London?

12 **fairy godmother**	gute Fee
13 **advice** [əd'vaɪs]	Ratschlag
17 **to seek one's fortune**	sein Glück suchen
19 **paved with gold**	mit Gold gepflastert

FARMER: Come on, then. It's a long way, so we must hurry before it gets dark.

Curtain.

(The storyteller exlains the next scene.)

Scene 2: The market

There is a bread and cake stall in the middle, a fruit stall on the left and on the right at the front near the audience a boot stall with a stool for people to sit on to try the boots. A scarf seller wanders through carrying her scarves on a tray. She has a mirror for people to see what they look like. Mr Fitzwarren and Alice go from stall to stall. There is a tall lady with her small husband who goes to buy a scarf. An old man wants to buy a pair of boots. Dick comes to look at the market and after a while he sees a thief at work.

MARKET STALL I: Fresh bread, fresh cakes! Fresh bread, fresh cakes! Baked this morning! No old stuff here!

STALL II: Apples and oranges! Apples and oranges! Come on! Get your vitamins from me and see how fit you can be!

STALL III: Brown boots! Black boots! The best boots in town! Why not give those old feet of yours a holiday!

OLD MAN: Have you got a pair of black boots, size 48?

STALL III: Certainly, sir!

Old man sits down to try them and the seller does not like the smell of the feet.

6 **(market) stall** Marktstand
8 **stool** Hocker
9 **tray** Tablett; *hier*: Bauchladen

STALL IV: Scarves! Scarves! Look at my beautiful scarves! I can make you look like a princess!

LARGE LADY: (*to small husband*) Wait a minute, Cecil, I must just try on this beautiful scarf! I want to look like a princess, too!

SMALL HUSBAND: (*behind his hand to audience*) She needs more than a scarf to make *her* look like a princess.

Scarf-seller gives her a mirror so that she can look at herself.

DICK: London is so big! So many streets! So many people! But wait! Look at that!

While he is watching, a thief goes behind Mr Fitzwarren, puts his hand into his pocket and steals a bag of gold. Dick runs after him, catches him and after a fight takes back the bag of money. The thief runs off and Dick gives the money back to Mr Fitzwarren who is standing now at the front of the stage in the centre.

MR FITZWARREN: (*shaking Dick's hand*) Thank you, thank you, young man! How lucky for me that you were here! Here, take this piece of gold for your trouble! Is there anything I can do for you?

DICK: Well, sir, I'm looking for work, sir, and somewhere to live. I don't know where to go in this big city.

ALICE: (*behind her hand to audience*) Now isn't that a yummy young man!

MR FITZWARREN.: Then come with us and I will ask our cook to give you work in the kitchen. This is my daughter, Alice.

Dick bows; Alice curtsies and smiles; then she winks at the audience.

18 **trouble** ['trʌbl]	*hier:* Mühe
22 **yummy** *(informal)*	lecker, toll
26 **to bow** [baʊ]	sich verbeugen
26 **to curtsey** ['kɜːtsɪ]	einen Knicks machen
26 **to wink**	mit den Augen zwinkern

Alice my dear, I'm sure we have an extra bed in the attic.

ALICE: Of course, father. (*taking Mr Fitzwarren's arm*) Why not, father? – Let's go, father!

SONG

Curtain.

(The storyteller explains the next scene.)

Scene 3: The kitchen at Mr Fitzwarren's house

Cook and Polly, the rather stupid servant, are on stage. Cook is examining what Polly is mixing in her bowl.

MRS SHUFFLEBOTTOM: (*drying her hands on a cloth*) Come on now! It's already 12 o'clock. Mr Fitzwarren and Alice will be back soon and they will want their lunch. What is this in this bowl? (*Trying it and not liking it*) But you have put far too much salt in this! It is terrible! When will you learn, you stupid thing?

POLLY: Oh, I can never do anything right in this house. (*behind her hand to the audience*) Silly old cow!

Enter Mr Fitzwarren, Alice and Dick. Cook and Polly curtsey.

MR FITZWARREN: Good morning, Mrs Shufflebottom. We're back again and I have brought a young man to help you and Polly in the kitchen. Now show him what he can do and where he can sleep. We will be upstairs. (*to Alice*) Come, my dear.

ALICE: Yes, Daddy darling! Good bye, Dicky-boy! See you later!

MR FITZWARREN: We hope you have something good for lunch. Ha!Ha! (*He rubs his tummy and licks his lips.*)

1	**attic**	Dachboden
9	**bowl** [bəʊl]	Schüssel
13	**to try s.th.**	*hier:* probieren
24	**tummy** (*informal*)	Bauch
24	**to lick**	lecken

Exit Mr Fitzwarren and Alice.

MRS SHUFFLEBOTTOM: Something good for lunch, he says! Not while this one here has her fingers in it! (*She hits Polly with a wooden spoon.*)

POLLY: Ouch! But you said I should be quick! I can never do anything right in this house!

MRS SHUFFLEBOTTOM: And now we have another idiot here!

She walks round him looking at him carefully.

Well, then, have you ever worked in a kitchen before, young man?

DICK: Well, no, ma'am, not really!

MRS SHUFFLEBOTTOM: Not really? Not really? We'll see about that! You can't be worse than this one here. (*She gives Polly a push.*)

POLLY: Ouch! Don't do that! I can never do anything right in this house!

MRS SHUFFLEBOTTOM: Now get these potatoes ready for lunch – and be quick!

Curtain.

(The storyteller explains the next scene.)

Scene 4: Dick's attic bedroom

The stage is dark. Enter Dick in his nightshirt and with a candle.

DICK: How dark it is in here!

He lies down in his bed and blows out the candle. Then there is a scratching noise as one rat appears, then another. King Rat appears and leads them in a circle to the music.

10 **ma'am** höfliche Form von 'madam'
12 **to give someone a push** jemanden schubsen
22 **to blow** [bləʊ] **out** auspusten
23 **scratching noise** Kratzgeräusch

If the group likes the idea, a dance routine could be organised – suggested background music: "Hall of the Mountain King" by Grieg. One pupil with a sign "Please boo!", another with a sign "Please hiss!" walk in front of the stage from one side to the other. Finally King Rat blows a whistle, the music stops and the rats crowd around Dick.

KING RAT: (*to audience shaking his fist*)
Riddle me ree, riddle me ree
Nothing is more terrible than me. (*going to Dick*)
Riddle me ree, riddle me roo
That's why I've come to frighten you!

Dick is very frightened and the rats crowd around him. Enter Fairy Bowbells from the side of the stage in front of the curtain.

FAIRY BOWBELLS: Oh, it's you again, is it? What do you think you're doing, King Rat? Frightening a poor boy so much?

KING RAT: (*to the audience*) Oh, not her again! (*to Fairy Bowbells*) Yes, and I will do what I like here in my own place, thank you very much!

Two or three voices at back of room

THREE VOICES: Oh no, you won't ...

KING RAT: (*to audience*) Oh yes, I will ...

THREE VOICES: Oh no, you won't ...

KING RAT: Oh yes, I will ...

BOWBELLS: Now, off with you before I do something really bad with my magic wand!

3	**to boo**	auspfeifen, ausbuhen
4	**to hiss**	(aus-)zischen
5	**finally** ['faɪnəlɪ]	am Ende, schließlich
5	**to blow a whistle**	auf einer Trillerpfeife pfeifen
7	**to shake a fist**	eine Faust ballen
8	**Riddle me ree, riddle me roo!**	(*Unsinnsreim*)
25	**magic wand** ['mædʒɪk 'wɒnd]	Zauberstab

Exit King Rat and Rat Chorus.

BOWBELLS: I'm sorry, Dick, but I can't come here every night. You must do something and I think the best idea for you is to get a cat.

DICK: I still have the piece of gold from Mr Fitzwarren. Tomorrow I will go to market again and see if I can buy a cat.

Curtain.

(The storyteller explains the next scene.)

Scene 5: Market

The same market stalls as before and a pet seller. People wander from stall to stall.

STALL III: Brown boots! Black boots! The best boots in town!
STALL II: Apples and Oranges! Apples and oranges!
STALL I: Come and buy my fresh bread! Lovely fresh cakes!
STALL IV: Scarves, beautiful scarves! Come and buy!
STALL V: Pussy cats and puppy dogs! Buy yourself a friend!

Enter Dick.

DICK: I'm lucky today. There's a woman selling small animals. I wonder if she has a cat for me. Tell me, good woman, do you have a cat for me, a quick and clever animal to catch all the rats which come to frighten me at night?

MARKET WOMAN: I think I have just the cat for you. She's a wonderful little rat-catcher – and beautiful, too. Look at her nice sharp claws!

1	**rat chorus**	Rattenchor
10	**pet seller**	Kleintierhändler
16	**pussy** ['pʊsɪ]	Kätzchen
16	**puppy** ['pʌpɪ]	Hundewelpe
24	**claw** [klɔː]	Kralle

She shows Puss and Puss shows her claws.

DICK: What a beautiful cat! How much do you want for her?

MARKET WOMAN: Well, for you, my dear, just one piece of gold will do.

DICK: Here you are and thank you! Come on, Puss, you have work to do!

SONG

Curtain.

(The storyteller explains the next scene.)

Scene 6: Dick's attic

Dick enters carrying a candle and Puss follows him.

DICK: Come on, Puss, this is where I sleep and here is a basket for you.

PUSS: Miaow! Miaow!

DICK: Good night, Puss, and sweet dreams! – But who knows what will happen if those rats come again.

Dick blows out candle and gets into bed. After a while the scratching starts and the rats appear one after the other – the same music as before – and go around in a circle to the music. Puss awakes and with one blow she hits each rat to the ground. Finally King Rat appears. The pupils carry the signs "Please boo!" and "Please hiss!" in front.

KING RAT:
Riddle me ree, riddle me ree,
Nothing is more terrible than me.
Riddle me ree, riddle me roo,
That's why I've come to frighten you.

3 **will do** *hier:* wird reichen
12 **basket** Korb
20 **blow** [bləʊ] Schlag

King Rat shakes his fist at the audience.

KING RAT: Oh! Oh! What have we here? A c - c - c - cat?

After a short fight with Puss he too falls to the floor.

DICK: Oh Puss! You are the best friend on earth! You've saved my life!

Puss shows her muscles to a short piece of music.

SONG (*e.g. "We are the Champions", Queen)*

Curtain.

(The storyteller explains the next scene.)

Scene 7: The kitchen

Mrs Shufflebottom, Polly and Dick are preparing a meal.

MRS SHUFFLEBOTTOM: Hurry up, you two lazybones! Nothing ready again und just today when the Captain is coming to visit Mr Fitzwarren. What do you call this mess here? (*She looks into Polly's bowl.*)

POLLY: Y-Y-Y-Yorkshire pudding!

MRS SHUFFLEBOTTOM: Yorkshire pudding? You must be joking!

POLLY: I can never do anything right in this house.

MRS SHUFFLEBOTTOM: (*to Dick*) And what do you think you are doing?

6	**to show one's muscles** ['mʌslz]	die Muskeln zeigen
11	**to prepare**	vorbereiten
12	**lazybones**	Faulpelz
14	**mess**	Schweinerei, Durcheinander
16	**Yorkshire pudding**	eine Art Pfannkuchen, die man in England zum Rinderbraten ißt

DICK: I'm chopping the carrots!

MRS SHUFFLEBOTTOM: You're murdering the carrots! How many times have I told you to cut them fine! See here – fine!

Enter Mr Fitzwarren, Captain Hornblower and Alice, and two sailors with a sack.

Oh, good morning, Mr Fitzwarren, sir, and Captain Hornblower.

Mrs Shufflebottom and Polly curtsey. The captain raises his hat.

MR FITZWARREN: Good morning, Mrs Shufflebottom, Polly, Dick. Here is Captain Hornblower. He is going on a long journey on one of my ships to Arabia to sell many beautiful things. He comes as usual to see if there is anything that you want to send for sale.

CAPTAIN HORNBLOWER: (*to Mrs Shufflebottom*) My good lady, how wonderful to see you again! When I am on the high seas I always dream of the fantastic dinners you give us here. (*to audience behind his hand*) What a woman, eh!

MRS SHUFFLEBOTTOM: Oh go on there, Captain Hornblower! But it's good that I finished that tablecloth I was making.

She gets it from the back and gives it to a sailor who puts it in the sack.

CAPTAIN HORNBLOWER: Wonderful, my little woman, wonderful! (*giving Mrs Shufflebottom a smack on her behind*)

Mr Fitzwarren: And you, Polly?

Polly brings something like a doll – e.g. a diddle doll or Teletubby.

1	**to chop**	hacken
2	**to murder**	ermorden, umbringen
7	**to raise o.'s hat**	den Hut ziehen
17	**go on there!**	hören Sie bloß auf!
18	**tablecloth**	Tischtuch
22	**to give someone a smack**	jemandem einen Klaps geben
22	**behind**	*hier:* Hintern

POLLY: Well, my auntie sent me this for my birthday. It's not quite what I wanted. I don't know, I can never do anything right in this house.

MR FITZWARREN: Why not? (*he puts the doll into the sack*)

MR FITZWARREN: How about you, Dick?

DICK: Well, I have nothing in the world to give, sir.

ALICE: But Dick, you must have something to send. All the servants send something.

DICK: All I have is my cat, sir, and she is very special.

MR FITZWARREN: Well, even a cat is better than nothing, Dick. Go and get her.

Dick goes and gets the cat and sadly gives Puss to the captain.

SONG

Curtain.

(The storyteller explains the next scene.)

Scene 8: The Sultan's palace

Before the curtain goes up, we hear the sound of Oriental music. The Sultan and his wife sit on beautiful cushions and the servants stand in the background. Enter the Grand Vizier. He bows.

GRAND VIZIER: We have visitors from a far off land, sire! Captain Hornblower is here again from England in his beautiful ship. He brings many rich and beautiful things for you to look at and perhaps buy. Shall I tell him that he may enter?

SULTAN: Why, certainly, my good servant. Tell him that I am happy to see him again.

18 **cushion** [ˈkʊʃən] Kissen
19 **Grand Vizier** [vɪˈzɪə] Minister im Dienste des Sultans (Wesir)
21 **sire** [saɪə] Anrede für einen König

Exit Grand Vizier. He comes back with Captain Hornblower followed by two sailors carrying a sack.

SULTAN: Greetings, o Captain from a far country. How was your long journey? Ah! I see you have brought us wonderful things to look at from your wonderful land.
CAPTAIN: Greetings, Sultan! Greetings, my lady! Yes, I have brought you some interesting things this time.

He shows things from the sack: Mrs Shufflebottom's cloth, Polly's doll etc.

SULTAN'S WIFE: Oh, what a beautiful cloth! Such fine and wonderful work! And this doll! Just fantastic! I've never seen anything like it in the world! We must have it for our children!
SULTAN: How much will you take for these things? One bag of gold? Two bags of gold?
CAPTAIN: Three bags of gold this time, Sultan.
SULTAN: But come, first we must have something to eat and drink!

The Sultan, his wife and captain Hornblower sit on the cushions. The Sultan claps his hands and the servants enter carrying food and drink. They put the things down and they start to eat. Then there is the scratching noise and out come the rats led by King Rat who this time wears a turban. They dance around in a circle to the music by Grieg. The two pupils with the boo and hiss signs appear. The Sultan's wife and the servants scream and run to the back of the stage.

KING RAT: (*Blows a whistle. The music stops and he comes to the front of the stage.*)

Riddle me ree, riddle me ree,
Cream cakes and jelly and ice-cream for tea.
Riddle me ree, riddle me roo,
Let's eat it all up in a minute or two!

3 **greetings** *hier:* seien Sie gegrüßt!
28 **jelly** ['dʒelɪ] Götterspeise

The rats eat all the food and then disappear when King Rat gives a sign.

SULTAN: (*He puts his arm round his wife and shakes his head. Comes back to the front of the stage with the others*) This is what happens every time we want to have something to eat. I would give half my kingdom if someone could only help us.
CAPTAIN: I think I have just what you need. Wait a minute.

He goes out and comes back with Puss.

SULTAN: What sort of animal is this? I have never seen one before.
CAPTAIN: This, o Sultan, is a cat and a wonderful rat-catcher, too. Let's have some more food!

The Sultan claps his hands. The Sultan, wife and captain Hornblower sit down. The servants bring food again. The rats appear and the Sultan and the others run to the back of the stage. The rats dance in a circle to the music. King Rat appears and the two pupils with the "boo" and "hiss" signs. King Rat blows the whistle. Music stops.

KING RAT: (*Coming to the front of the stage and speaking to the audience*) Riddle me ree, riddle me ree!
Cream cakes and jelly and ice-cream for tea!
Riddle me ree, riddle me roo!
Let's eat it all up in a minute or two!

He and the rats want to eat up all the food but Puss appears and hits the rats to the ground.

KING RAT: (*to Puss*) Haven't we met somewhere before?
PUSS: Miaow! Miaow! (*She hits him to the ground.*)

3 **to shake** schütteln
6 **kingdom** Königreich

SULTAN: (*running up to the front of the stage to the cat*) Puss, you Wonder-Puss! You have saved us! – Captain Hornblower! (*shaking Captain Hornblower's hand*) How can I ever thank you? I said I would give half my kingdom to the one who helps us. And that I will do. (*clapping his hands*) Gold! Bring gold for the captain!

Servants enter with sacks of gold.

SONG (e.g. "We are the champions")

Curtain.

(The storyteller explains the next scene.)

Scene 9: The kitchen of Mr Fitzwarren's house

Polly is polishing the silver on the right of the stage. Mrs Shufflebottom is mixing something in a bowl in the centre. Dick is sitting on a stool on the left, cleaning his shoes.

MRS SHUFFLEBOTTOM: Captain Hornblower has come back from his long journey to Arabia and is coming to dinner tonight. We must have something special. Dick, go and get the potatoes! ... Dick! Dick! What are you doing? (*coming down to Dick on the left*) Cleaning your shoes? In my nice kitchen? (*taking him by the ear*) What do you think you are doing? (*hitting him with her wooden spoon*) Now, off with you and get those potatoes!

DICK: Do this, do that, do this, do that! What must I do next?

POLLY: Yes, and I can never do anything right in this house!

MRS SHUFFLEBOTTOM: (*to Polly*) You, be quiet, or else you'll be sorry! Now where are those potatoes?

12 **to polish** polieren, putzen

Dick gets up and leaves. Soon there is the sound of things falling behind the scene. Someone can throw a bag of empty tins on the floor. Dick enters looking miserable with a bowl on his head.

DICK: I think the pudding fell on me.

MRS SHUFFLEBOTTOM: The pudding fell on you? That's it! That's it! That's the last time you make a mess in my kitchen! You idiot boy! You don't know a carrot from a cabbage! You're useless! Away with you and don't come back again! (*shaking her wooden spoon at him*)

Curtain.

DICK: (*coming in front of the curtain carrying his stick with his belongings and looking sad*) What am I to do? What am I to do? I can't stay here any longer! I've no money and no friends – no good Puss to be at my side and keep those horrible rats away from my room. Mrs Shufflebottom always hated me and Polly was no help! So now I'll just have to go back to where I came from.

SONG (e.g. "Always look on the bright side of life" – Monty Python)

Dick walks round the audience to the music. Music dies down. Dick appears in front of the curtain carrying his stick with his belongings over his shoulder. There is a signpost showing the way to Highgate Hill, London, and the North. Dick takes the way to the North. Then suddenly he hears church bells. Two or three voices chant in the background with the bells.

3	**miserable** ['mɪzrəbl]	unglücklich, jämmerlich
7	**cabbage** ['kæbɪdʒ]	Kohl
12	**belongings**	Hab und Gut
22	**signpost**	Wegweiser
25	**to chant** [tʃɑ:nt]	im Chor sprechen

VOICES: Turn again, Whittington! Turn again, Whittington, Lord Mayor of London! (*Repeat!*)

Enter Fairy Bowbells also in front of curtain.

BOWBELLS: Dick, what are you doing?

DICK: Oh, Fairy Bowbells, how glad I am to see you! I can't stand it anymore! I haven't got a friend in the world and Mrs Shufflebottom has treated me so badly. Even my cat has gone! I'm leaving and going back to the North.

BOWBELLS: But Dick, don't you hear the bells, the Bow bells?

Dick listens again. The bells ring and the voices chant again.

VOICES: Turn again, Whittington! Turn again, Whittington! Three times Lord Mayor of London!

DICK: What does that mean? Lord Mayor of London?

BOWBELLS: Don't you see, Dick? You must go back! The bells are calling you! Go back and find out what they are trying to tell you!

Exit Dick and Fairy Bowbells.

(The storyteller explains the next scene.)

Scene 10: Mr Fitzwarren's house

Mr Fitzwarren sits in a chair at the front left of stage. Alice stands behind the chair. Captain Hornblower stands on the right.

MR FITZWARREN: How happy I am, my good friend, that you have arrived back safely and that the journey went well. How did the Sultan like the things we sent?

1	**to turn**	*hier:* zurückgehen
1	**Lord Mayor**	Bürgermeister
7	**to treat**	behandeln
9	**Bow bells**	die Glocken der Kirche von Bow (in London)

CAPTAIN HORNBLOWER: He took them all, sir, and gladly.

MR FITZWARREN: Alice, my dear, ask Mrs Shufflebottom and Polly to come. They must hear the good news, too.

Exit Alice.

CAPTAIN HORNBLOWER: (*to audience behind his hand*) Ah! Mrs Shufflebottom! What a woman, eh! Em! I had a little question I wanted to ask her but ...

Enter Alice with Mrs Shufflebottom and Polly.

CAPTAIN HORNBLOWER: (*bowing*) Mrs Shufflebottom, my dear lady, how wonderful to see you again. You look great, my dear! And Polly!

Mrs Shufflebottom and Polly curtsey.

MRS SHUFFLEBOTTOM: Why, Captain Hornblower, I hear you have good news for us.

CAPTAIN HORNBLOWER: Yes, my dear, the Sultan and his good lady loved the things you sent ...

MRS SHUFFLEBOTTOM: Did you show him my tablecloth?

CAPTAIN: I did indeed, Mrs Shufflebottom, and they all thought it was a beautiful piece of work!

POLLY: Did he like my doll?

CAPTAIN: Indeed he did!

POLLY: (*jumping about*) Oh yippee! He liked my doll! He liked my doll!

CAPTAIN: He wanted to keep everything and sent a good price for all. But the most wonderful thing for the Sultan was ... the cat!

ALL: (*together*) The cat?

CAPTAIN: Yes, the cat! Your kitchen boy, Dick, sent his cat and it was just what the Sultan needed. For years rats have overrun his

1	**gladly**	gern
18	**indeed**	in der Tat
22	**yippee!**	*Freudenschrei*
28	**to overrun**	*hier:* bevölkern

palace. Every time they had a meal the rats came and ate everything up! It was quite terrible! Now there is that brave puss to look after everything and keep the palace rat-free. He has paid many sacks of gold for the cat. Dick is now a rich man! But where is he? (*He looks around.*)

ALICE: (*coming to the front, holding out her hands*) Dick! My Dick! Where are you, my darling?

MR FITZWARREN: Where is Dick, Mrs Shufflebottom?

MRS SHUFFLEBOTTOM: (*carefully*) Well, we had a bit of a misunderstanding, as you might say!

POLLY: Yes, I can never do anything right in this house and he can't either.

Enter Dick. He goes to the centre. Everybody looks happy and crowds round Dick.

MR FITZWARREN: Dick, my boy!

ALICE: Dick, my darling!

POLLY: You're back!

CAPTAIN: Well! Well! Well!

MRS SHUFFLEBOTTOM: Now, there's a thing!

DICK: (*coming to Mr Fitzwarren*) I was on my way back to the North. I was so unhappy, sir, without my cat. But then I heard the sound of the church bells, the Bow bells, sir, and they seemed to tell me to come back.

Enter Fairy Bowbells waving her magic wand.

FAIRY BOWBELLS: Yes, indeed, they told you to come back, Dick! You are a rich man!

DICK: What? I don't believe it!

CAPTAIN: Yes, my boy, the Sultan has paid many sacks of gold for your cat, the clever rat-catcher!

2 **brave** tapfer
9 **misunderstanding** Mißverständnis
10 **as you might say** sozusagen

FAIRY BOWBELLS: And you shall become three times Lord Mayor of London!

DICK: (*putting his hand to his head*) Am I dreaming?

ALICE: (*running to him and taking his hand*) No, you are not dreaming, my darling! We are together again. Now we can be married! (*to Mr Fitzwarren*) Is that not true, father dear?

MR FITZWARREN: (*getting up and putting his arms round them both*) How happy I am!

CAPTAIN: (*going down on one knee in front of Mrs Shufflebottom*) That is just the little question that I wanted to pop to you, my little woman!

Mrs Shufflebottom falls down flat on the stage in shock! Polly tries to bring her back to life by waving her apron over her. Captain Hornblower looks very worried.

FAIRY BOWBELLS: (*coming to the centre*) So you see everything has turned out for the best, and they all live happily ever after.

SONG

Curtain.

10 **to pop the question**	einen Heiratsantrag stellen
13 **to wave**	*hier:* wedeln
13 **apron** ['eɪprən]	Schürze
16 **to turn out for the best**	sich zum Besten wenden

The storyteller's text

Scene 2

Dick wundert sich über das rege Treiben in der Großstadt London – es gibt so viel zu sehen. Entsetzt ist er, als er einen Dieb ertappt, der gerade die Geldbörse eines reichen Londoner Kaufmanns stehlen will. Dieser Herr, Mr Fitzwarren, zeigt sich sehr dankbar für Dicks Hilfe. Er gibt ihm ein Goldstück und bietet ihm eine Stellung in seinem Haushalt als Küchenjunge an. Mr Fitzwarren ist nicht nur ein sehr reicher Mann, er hat auch eine sehr hübsche Tochter!

Scene 3

Mrs Shufflebottom, die Köchin in Mr Fitzwarrens Haus, ist leider nicht sehr freundlich, und Polly, das Küchenmädchen, ist keine Intelligenzbestie. Und Dick? Dick selber hat so gut wie keine Erfahrung mit Küchenarbeiten. Das stimmt Mrs Shufflebottom natürlich auch nicht freundlicher.

Scene 4

Die Dachkammer, in der Dick schlafen muss, ist nicht sehr gemütlich; sie ist dunkel und nachts wimmelt es dort von Ratten. Schon in der ersten Nacht hat Dick ein furchtbares Erlebnis: es erscheint der Rattenkönig! Wenn Sie in dieser Szene Dick helfen wollen, dann buhen Sie und zischen und zeigen dem Rattenpack Ihre ganze Abneigung! Fairy Bowbells, die gute Fee, muss eingreifen, und sie rät Dick, sich am nächsten Tag auf dem Markt eine Katze zu kaufen.

Scene 5

Dick folgt dem Rat von Fairy Bowbells und geht am Morgen nach dieser schrecklichen Nacht zum Markt. Und er hat Glück! An diesem Morgen ist da auch eine Marktfrau, die Kleintiere verkauft, und sie hat eine wunderbare Katze, mit scharfen Krallen, genau so, wie man sie zum Fangen von Ratten braucht. Dick kauft sie und bezahlt sie mit dem Goldstück, das er als Belohnung von Mr Fitzwarren bekommen hatte.

Scene 6
Dick und Puss, die Katze, machen es sich in Dicks Kammer, so weit es möglich ist, gemütlich. Aber in der nächsten Nacht das gleiche Spektakel! Wieder erscheint der Rattenkönig mit seiner widerlichen Truppe! (Vergessen Sie nicht, ihm Ihre Gefühle zu zeigen! Buhen und zischen Sie!) Aber dieses Mal ist Dick nicht allein! Seine Katze Puss lässt ihre Muskeln spielen!

Scene 7
In der Küche herrscht große Aufregung! Mr Fitzwarren erwartet seinen guten alten Bekannten Captain Hornblower als Gast, und Mrs Shufflebottom weiß, wie sehr der Captain ihre Kochkünste schätzt. (Oder vielleicht auch ein bisschen mehr als nur die!) Der Captain hat vor, mit seinem Schiff und reicher Ladung nach Arabien zu segeln, um dort Geschäfte zu machen. Jeder darf sich an seinen Geschäften beteiligen und ihm etwas mitgeben. Nur Dick hat Probleme. Er ist ein armer Junge und besitzt absolut nichts, was er dem Captain mitgeben könnte. Nur mit schwerem Herzen trennt er sich schließlich von Puss, seiner Katze.

Scene 8
Für den Sultan in Arabien ist Captain Hornblower ein gern gesehener Gast. Der Sultan und seine Frau sind auch dieses Mal wieder beeindruckt von den fremden Sachen, die der Captain ihnen anbietet. Der Handel läuft gut, aber das anschließende Festessen wird brutal gestört durch King Rat und seine widerliche Rattenbande. Kaum stehen die köstlichen Speisen bereit, da fallen auch schon die ungebetenen Gäste über sie her. Der Sultan klagt dem Captain sein Leid, denn das geschehe jedes Mal, wenn Essen serviert würde. Ein halbes Königreich verspricht er demjenigen, der ihn von der Rattenplage befreien könnte. Aber der Captain weiß Rat und holt vom Schiff Dicks Katze Puss zur Hilfe. Und

wieder lässt Puss ihre Muskeln spielen! Der Sultan ist begeistert und sein Dank fürstlich.

Scene 9
Wieder herrscht große Aufregung im Hause von Mr Fitzwarren. Captain Hornblower wird zurückerwartet, und Mrs Shufflebottom will natürlich mit ihren Kochkünsten einen guten Eindruck machen. Dick stellt sich ungeschickt an, Mrs Shufflebottom verliert die Nerven und jagt ihn aus dem Haus. Dick will London wieder verlassen, aber auf dem Weg nach Norden kommt er nicht weit. Kurz hinter Holloway hört er die Kirchenglocken von London, und diese scheinen ihm eine unglaubliche Botschaft mitzuteilen. Auch Fairy Bowbells kommt und hilft Dick, die märchenhafte Botschaft der Kirchenglocken zu verstehen, die da lautet:
Kehre um, Whittington! Dreimal Bürgermeister von London!

Scene 10
Captain Hornblower hat für alle gute Nachrichten. Alle mitgegebenen Sachen hat er für einen guten Preis verkaufen können. Aber als er von Dicks Katze berichtet, ihrer Heldentat und den Säcken von Gold, die nun Dick gehören werden, bemerkt er, dass dieser fehlt. Aber die Ratlosigkeit ist nicht von langer Dauer. Dick erscheint im richtigen Moment, auch Fairy Bowbells mit ihrem Zauberstab. Dick ist nun reich, und eine große Karriere als Bürgermeister von London liegt vor ihm. Alice ist überglücklich und hört bereits die Hochzeitsglocken läuten, und auch der Captain kommt endlich dazu, Mrs Shufflebottom einen Heiratsantrag zu machen, auf den diese in ganz besonderer Weise reagiert.

Questions and exercises

Scene 1: Farmer Brown's farm

A: Which is right?

1. Farmer Brown is angry because
   a) the cows don't give milk
   b) the workers are all on holiday
   c) Dick can't carry a sack of potatoes
   d) Dick has lost his pitchfork again.

2. Dick is unhappy because
   a) he must put all the potatoes into the sacks
   b) he has no friends and family to help him
   c) Farmer Green does not want to take him with him
   d) Fairy Bowbells never comes to visit him.

3. Fairy Bowbells tells Dick
   a) that he has often seen her before
   b) that he must make new friends
   c) that he should hurry and go home before it gets dark
   d) that he should go to London to look for a new life.

B: Answer the questions

1) Can you give three reasons why Dick should go to London?
2) Write as many words as possible for things you can see or find on a farm. Compare your list with your partner's.

Scene 2: The market

A: Are these sentences right or wrong? If they are wrong, correct them.

1. The fruit seller tells the people that fruit is good for them.
2. The old man asks the boot seller to repair his old boots.

3. The large lady tries the scarf because she wants to buy her daughter a birthday present.
4. The large lady's husband thinks she looks like a princess.
5. Dick sees how a thief steals Mr Fitzwarren's bag of gold.
6. Mr Fitzwarren shakes Dick's hand because he has not met him before.
7. Alice really likes Dick.
8. Mr Fitzwarren says that Dick can come with them and he will ask the gardener to give him work in the garden.

B: Answer the questions

1) Can you think of market stalls which sell other things? What could these market people shout to make people buy their things?
2) In modern times, what kind of shop would you go to for: bread and cakes / fruit / boots / scarves ?
3) Imagine that you are the thief and that you want to tell your friends what happened in the market. Write the dialogue.

Scene 3: The kitchen at Mr Fitzwarren's house

A: Find the right word

1. Mr Fitzwarren and Alice will soon be back for their
   a) supper
   b) lunch
   c) breakfast.

2. Mrs Shufflebottom thinks Polly is
   a) a very clever cook
   b) a big help in the kitchen
   c) a stupid thing.

3. Mrs Shufflebottom is angry with Polly because she has used too much
   a) sugar
   b) soap
   c) salt.

4. Polly says that
   a) she really loves her work
   b) she can never do anything right
   c) she thinks Mrs Shufflebottom is great.

5. Mr Fitzwarren has brought Dick to help
   a) Mrs Shufflebottom in the kitchen
   b) Alice in the house
   c) the neighbour in his garden.

6. Mrs Shufflebottom says that if she thinks of Polly in the kitchen, then Dick
   a) must be better
   b) can't be worse
   c) must be as bad.

B: Answer the questions

1) Mrs Shufflebottom wants to make "something good for lunch". What do you like for lunch? Tell your partner three things!
2) Dick and Polly must help in the kitchen. What kind of things do you think they must do? How do you help in the kitchen?
3) What things do you find in a modern kitchen that Mrs Shufflebottom has never heard of?

Scene 4: Dick's attic bedroom

A: Which is right?

1. Dick can't sleep because
   a) it is very noisy outside

b) he's eaten too much
c) he hears a scratching noise.

2. Dick is frightened because
   a) he thinks the thief is in the house
   b) the rats come into the room
   c) Mrs Shufflebottom is coming up the stairs.

3. Fairy Bowbells is angry because
   a) King Rat is coming to frighten Dick
   b) King Rat never knocks before he comes into the room
   c) King Rat didn't ask her to his party.

B: Answer the questions

1) Were you ever frightened? Did someone help you? Tell your partner about it.
2) Think up a little story about how you went to bed one night and lay in the dark. Suddenly there was a scratching noise at the window and you got up and opened it. Go on!

Scene 5: The market *and* ***Scene 6: Dick's attic***

A: Which is right?

1. The boot stall is selling
   a) brown boots and black shoes
   b) brown shoes and black boots
   c) brown boots and black boots.

2. The woman at the pet stall says that
   a) the cat can do clever tricks
   b) the cat has got sharp claws
   c) the cat likes to drink milk.

3. When Puss is in Dick's room
   a) she has a fight with all the rats
   b) she chases all the rats away
   c) King Rat frightens her.

B: Answer the questions

1) The pet seller at the market sells young cats and dogs. What other animals could she sell?
2) What other animals could she **not** sell there?
3) Imagine you are one of the rats who was lucky enough to get away. Tell your rat friends what happened in Dick's attic room.

Scene 7: The kitchen

A: Are these sentences right or wrong?
If they are wrong, correct them.

1. Mr Fitzwarren is going to visit Captain Hornblower on his ship with Alice.
2. Polly is chopping the carrots and Dick is making a vanilla pudding.
3. Captain Hornblower loves Mrs Shufflebottom's meals.
4. Captain Hornblower is sailing to America soon to buy many things.
5. Polly has made a tablecloth and wants to give it to Captain Hornblower.
6. Dick says that he has only his cat to send for sale.
7. Mr Fitzwarren thinks it is a silly idea to send a cat.

B: Answer the questions

1) Polly is trying to make Yorkshire pudding. What can you make, bake or cook?
2) Captain Hornblower is going to Arabia. Which names of countries do you know? Which would you like to visit and why?

3) To **make** or to **do**?
   (For example: to **make** a tablecloth, to **do** homework)
   What fits what? Make a list!

a cake	the shopping	a list	some work	a model ship
your homework	the washing-up	a meal	jobs in the garden	a mistake
a dress				

Scene 8: The Sultan's palace

A: Complete the sentences

1. The Grand Vizier comes to tell the Sultan and his wife that Captain Hornblower ...
2. Captain Hornblower says that he has brought ...
3. The Sultan's wife thinks that the tablecloth is ...
4. The captain wants ... for the beautiful things.
5. The Sultan tells Captain Hornblower that they must first ...
6. Then suddenly rats run in and ...
7. Captain Hornblower goes and gets ... because she is ...
8. The Sultan is so happy that he wants to give Captain Hornblower ...

B: Answer the questions

1) British children like to eat jelly (*Götterspeise, Wackelpudding*) and ice cream at parties. What do you like to eat and drink at a party?
2) The Grand Vizier told his wife later about the meeting between the Sultan and Captain Hornblower. What did he say? Write the dialogue.

Scene 9: The kitchen

A: Which is right?

1. Dick is busy cleaning
   a) the silver
   b) his shoes
   c) his football boots.

2. Mrs Shufflebottom says that for dinner that night they must have
   a) potatoes and carrots
   b) Mr Fitzwarren's favourite meal
   c) something special.

3. Mrs Shufflebottom is so angry that she hits Dick
   a) with her wooden spoon
   b) with a stick
   c) on the head with a plate.

4. Dick says that the ... fell on him.
   a) potatoes
   b) pudding
   c) plates.

5. Dick wants to go back to
   a) the market
   b) the City of London
   c) the North.

6. Fairy Bowbells tells him to listen to
   a) the church bells
   b) his friends
   c) the radio.

7. The Bow bells say that Dick will be Lord Mayor of London
   a) once
   b) twice
   c) three times.

B: Answer the questions

1) Dick is alone again. He misses Puss. Imagine Puss could send him a postcard from Arabia. What would she write?
2) Look at the adjectives below. Which are right to describe Mrs Shufflebottom – Polly – Dick – Fairy Bowbells? And why?

(*For example:* Fairy Bowbells is **kind** because she helps Dick.)

excited	sad	worried	frightened	nice	funny
angry	stupid	kind	silly	miserable	

Scene 10: Mr Fitzwarren's house

A: Is everything right in these sentences? If not, correct them.

1. Captain Hornblower tells them that the Sultan liked most of the things he took with him to Arabia.
2. Alice goes to get Mrs Shufflebottom and Polly so that they can hear the good news, too.
3. Captain Hornblower tells them that the Sultan took Mrs Shufflebottom's doll and Polly's tablecloth.
4. The Sultan wanted to keep the cat because she was a wonderful pet for his children.
5. Dick is now a rich man because the Sultan paid many sacks of gold for the cat.
6. Dick comes back because he has forgotten something.
7. Mr Fitzwarren wants to marry Mrs Shufflebottom.
8. Fairy Bowbells says that now everything will be alright.

B: Answer the questions

1) Imagine **you** are Polly. What would you tell your mother about Mrs Shufflebottom and life in the kitchen? Write a little dialogue.
2) Dick's cat is now living with the rich Sultan. Describe a day in her new life.

3) The real Dick Whittington did a lot to help other people when he became rich. If you had a lot of money, what would you do to help the people in your town?

After reading the play

1) What did you think of the pantomime?
I liked / didn't like "Dick Whittington" because ...
My favourite character was ... because ...
The best part was when ...
2) Draw a poster for the pantomime. Hang it up in the classroom and choose the best. You can design a programme too!